Index

Technical Analysis 3

   Chapter 1 - What is Technical Analysis 7

      1.1 – The basic assumptions of Technical Analysis 11

      1.2 – What do prices mean and how do they move? 18

      1.3 – The market cycle model 29

      1.4 – Financial markets 35

      1.5 – The various theories of Technical Analysis 43

   Chapter 2 - Dow's Theory 51

      2.1 – The six fundamental points of Dow's Theory 54

      2.2 – Bulls and bears in the financial market...72

      3.1 – The most important graphs 81

3.2 – The main technical oscillators 96

3.3 – Market indicators 110

Technical Analysis

The financial market can be particularly advantageous for all those investors who decide to base their strategy on some principles that have historically led to success. In particular, the traders who over the years have managed to distinguish themselves from the others are those who have identified some market reversals in advance, acting accordingly. The Technical Analysis is really focused on the study of the behaviors that can provoke a tendential inversion. Initially the principles contained in it were applied only within the stock market. Today, on the other hand, Technical Analysis is applied, sometimes with great success, also to bond markets, currency markets and commodity markets.

The technical analyst must, however, become estranged from all the other subjects present on the market, he must assume ideas that contrast with the positions assumed by the majority of the traders and must focus his analysis on hypothetically valid forecasts of the market trend. Acting in this way on the market, however, requires particular aptitude and above all commitment and constancy. The study phase of the market could prove to be exhausting but, thanks to information technology and technology, this step can now be made easier and faster.

Despite the aid provided by the graphs, indicators and oscillators, the technical analyst must be able to interpret the market, must know the assumptions on which to base his strategy and must create a personal system that allows him to manage his capital rationally and the risk inherent in trading activity.

The Technical Analysis therefore allows to have a solid base on which to base one's investments, with a guarantee of success, if correctly applied, rather broad.

Chapter 1 - What is Technical Analysis

Like any method of analysis and every investment strategy within a financial market, even Technical Analysis must not be imagined as an infallible tool, capable of generating constant profits without running any risk. This analysis also presents many advantages and defects, and requires a study and an application in the subject that can be very expensive, both from an economic point of view and from a personal point of view, as it requires time and a lot of effort. At the same time, if applied accurately, if accompanied by an excellent risk management strategy and an equally positive capital management strategy, the Technical Analysis can be effective. Of course, for every investor, the best way to achieve success in trading is to combine, blend and harmonize multiple types of analysis, in particular Technical Analysis and Fundamental Analysis, in order to exploit the strengths of each , trying to fill the gaps, however indelible.

The Technical Analysis bases its approach to the world of trading and financial markets on the statistical and analytical study of historical trends and developments shown by the trends observed in past periods, in order to obtain important information that can help the trader to understand what the likely future trend in price levels will be. Therefore the objective of this analysis is not to provide an instantaneous method capable of generating profits, but rather to enrich the trader with news, information and awareness that will allow him to study the best possible approach to the market and to expand his own know how.

In this way the technical analyst will be able not only to understand what is actually happening on the financial markets at a given moment, but also to go back to the reasons that have caused a certain fluctuation in the price level. It is only in this way, having a clear and complete view of the entire market and its evolution, that the trader can enter more deeply into the mechanisms that move and modify each asset, discovering what the links and relationships are that each instrument financial links with the subjects and other elements present both inside and outside the market, increasing its chances of achieving success and, consequently, of remaining on the market in the medium and long term.

1.1 – The basic assumptions of Technical Analysis

Each Technical Analysis must be based on certain assumptions, necessary for the trader in order to find the right operating method that must be adapted according to his own strategy and that must be set on the set objectives.

First of all, a correct Technical Analysis must be based on the idea that the oscillations on the market are the result of a constant ideological and pragmatic battle fought between buyers and sellers. This incessant struggle has a fundamental consequence, namely that the market discounts everything. This means that the price movement already includes all the social, political, economic and ideological factors that have influenced its evolution. Furthermore, this assumption implies that the oscillation that each trader can observe on a financial market is absolutely not the result of chance, but is due to the set of actions put into practice by the active subjects, in a constant, sudden and above all voluntary manner.

That said, the first assumption of the Technical Analysis is based on the concept that the analyst must neither seek nor understand what are the motivations that led to a given oscillation, because these are already implicit in the bargaining that took place previously between sellers and buyers. And it is precisely in this sense that it is possible to affirm that the market discounts everything.

A second assumption can be identified in the idea that every movement that takes place within the market is the result of a law, more physical than financial, of cause and effect. In this sense, any similar price movement can be traced back to a similar cause, which tends to repeat itself over time. The subjects present in the market, in fact, act in a repetitive manner, not being able to control their own attitudes. This means that the history of a trend tends to repeat itself over time, although it would be more correct to say that it is the attitudes of traders and the various bargains that repeat themselves, thus generating similar fluctuations.

Finally, there is a third prerequisite, fundamental for every trader to implement a correct technical analysis. This is the concept of the validity of trends, which leads investors to think that it is more correct to imagine that the trend continues in the direction taken obstinately, until a clear signal is identified that identifies a trend reversal. This assumption is followed to the letter especially by a particular type of trader, known as trend following, which tend to chase the trend without ever trying to anticipate a possible trend reversal.

In addition to the three fundamental assumptions of Technical Analysis, there are concepts that every investor must not neglect, even if these may appear obvious. In fact it is known to all that the financial market is inefficient. This means that the negotiations between the two parties responsible for price level fluctuations do not always lead to optimal results for both parties. Generally, in fact, one of the two forces prevails over the other, generating oscillations that induce prices to clearly disadvantage the weak part of the relationship. Rarely, however, the forces of the two parties are equivalent, leading to the achievement of the optimal price level in the market. This scenario would represent a unique opportunity for every trader, who could invest following the effectiveness of the market.

A second concept can be found in the idea that the market, in addition to being ineffective, is also irrational. In fact, the subjects that participate in it are often moved by feelings that lead to error, generating unpredictable fluctuations in the price level. A trader who goes through a long negative phase, for example, is induced to increase his investment, knowing that sooner or later this trend will have to end. Every action carried out in the market therefore follows human irrationality, often leading to trivial or otherwise avoidable errors. For this reason, many traders try to eliminate the emotional element from their trading strategy by relying on fully automated systems, which base their investments only on objective data and statistics, tending to optimize the relationship between return and risk.

1.2 – What do prices mean and how do they move?

The main characteristic of the Technical Analysis, which distinguishes it from all other types of analysis, consists precisely in the interpretation of the market as an incessant financial battle between buyers and sellers. This view necessarily shifts attention not to the factors that influence the various market fluctuations, but directly to prices. The objective is instead to deduce the likely advantageous purchases or profitable sales of the positions opened by the traders, depending on the predicted scenario.

The same oscillation, seen by the technical analyst as a consequence of the battle between active subjects of the market, can be interpreted by the fundamental analyst as an effect of corporate communications, which may concern the conclusion of a specific business process, or simply the publication of a balance sheet , whether positive or negative, at the end of the year. The cassettista investor, instead, will see the oscillation as a consequence of the change in the inflation rate. This does not mean, however, that one procedure is better than another, but that interpretations within the financial market can be multiple, all dictated by correct concepts, but each of which has flaws, due essentially to the impossibility of being able to predict the future.

Through the use of a technical analysis, therefore, the trader is urged to examine the individual price levels and the graphs that contain them, basing his study on a solid statistical and mathematical basis, in order to identify inconsistencies that could alter the trend upwards or downwards. Precisely for this reason, the Technical

Analysis requires the investor a particular effort in the period that anticipates the entry and exit from the market, but also a greater propensity to risk compared to the traditional trader, supported however by a greater awareness of the mechanism on the market and understanding of all the processes that are affecting the trend fluctuation. Furthermore, the technical analyst must show himself to be even more dynamic and active than all the other analysts, and this depends precisely on the methodology with which he approaches the market.

The Technical Analysis is however criticized by many experts in the world of trading, especially due to one of its main assumptions. In fact, according to many critics, it is not correct to think that every financial event can be discounted in prices. The graphs, even following this logic, would still not be able to understand in advance the future price fluctuations, but would offer the trader only a snapshot image of the market situation.

This can actually be corrected in part: many professional traders rely on Technical Analysis, obtaining excellent results even in the long term, which is why it is reasonable to think that this type of analysis, supported by good capital management strategies and risk, may work.

The Technical Analysis, naturally, bases its roots in the idea of trend, understood as a qualitative measure of the price level and its evolution, in a given time interval. Analysts identify three trends, namely the primary one, the intermediate one and the short term one.

1.2.1 – Primary trend

A trend is defined as primary when its trend develops constantly in a time interval that varies from one to two years. This is the trend that stubbornly follows the so-called trend following. It can be either upward or downward and occurs both in stock and bond markets, and in commodity markets. The theoretical model of a primary trend presents an initial ascending phase which, once the maximum point is reached, continues in a new downward trend of equal duration with respect to the first. In reality these durations do not always coincide, and generally traders open their positions following the primary trend without assuming a possible direction reversal.

1.2.2 – Intermediate trend

The primary trend, both in its ascending and descending phases, does not show a linear trend, but fluctuates continuously on the basis of the reactions of the active subjects present on the market. These oscillations are called intermediate trends and are defined as countercyclical tendencies within the primary trend. They have a much shorter duration than the primary trend, as it is possible to observe the intermediate trends for periods ranging from three weeks to six months. The traders study the intermediate trends both to obtain profits in the medium term, and to take advantage of some advantages offered by short-term trades, profitable especially if carried out on the real estate sector, but not only. The intermediate trend is in fact kept constantly under observation by traders who want to identify any signs of a probable slowdown in the strength of the trend that would result in a possible turnaround.

1.2.3 – Short term trends

In turn, even intermediate trends can be interrupted and altered by small and short-term fluctuations. These fluctuations, defined as short-term trends, can last up to a maximum of four weeks. These types of trends are difficult to identify and are influenced by random social, political and economic events. Naturally, a trader tends to identify short-term trends that last at least three weeks, while those of shorter duration, besides being more difficult to identify, do not offer sufficient guarantees to make a profitable investment.

1.3 – The market cycle model

In a financial market, therefore, prices are influenced by different trends, and it is essential for a technical analyst to identify which is the most important of these, so that it can be monitored over time. Specifically, trend following are especially interested in events that can influence the trend of the primary trend, but at the same time they cannot completely exclude the monitoring of intermediate trends, which could still offer important information on the strength possessed by the primary trend. For this kind of investors it is in fact fundamental to try to understand what is the maturity level of the primary trend. To do this it is important to delve into the relationships between intermediate trends and short-term trends, so as to understand how and with what entities they are able to influence the primary trend.

Conversely, the subjects who decide to invest in the futures markets analyze mainly the short-term trends, as they base their profits on the minimum fluctuations in the price level. However, they can only successfully invest once they understand the direction taken by the primary trend and the one taken by any intermediate trends on the market. The need to fully understand the entire market lies in the fact that short-term trends show a greater excursion when they follow the same direction as the primary or intermediate trend. Conversely, traders record the greatest losses when the short-term trend shows an opposite trend to that possessed by the primary trend and the intermediate trend.

All of this falls within the market cycle model and indicates how important and at the same time it is difficult to analyze a market. Understanding the market is in fact fundamental both for a technical analyst inclined to invest in the long term, known as an investor, and for an analyst inclined to short-term investment, known as a trader.

With the advent of personal computers and technology, traders have seen the way to enter the market become simpler. In fact, the Internet allows trading to be carried out from anywhere, with the sole requirement of having a sufficiently stable connection, in real time: in this way the trader can invest quickly based on market analysis. It is therefore possible to apply the principles underlying the Technical Analysis to the intra-day and short-term trends on the market.

Of course there are differences between intra-day trends and long-term trends. First of all, a possible trend reversal in the intra-day trend would have little relevance for the purposes of a change in the primary trend. A second difference lies in the fact that the very short-term trends are much more susceptible to the economic news and the reactions of the other subjects present on the market. Consequently, it is possible to identify in these trends a much higher volatility which, in addition to facilitating the insights on the trend of the market, allows investors to pay much less attention to the study of prices than that required by long-term trends.

More primary trends form the so-called long-term trend. This is defined in technical jargon as a secular trend and develops over a very long time span, which can even reach twenty-five years. Once this "secular" trend has been identified, investors can act on primary trends in the same way traders act on intra-day trends: primary trends, in fact, increase their intensity if their trend follows that of the secular trend, while slowing down their trend if the direction taken is opposite to that of very long-term trends.

1.4 – Financial markets

The financial markets and the trends of the financial instruments contained in them are closely linked to the expectations placed in the evolution of the economy by investors, but also to the direct effects that economic developments can have on the price of a given financial product and even to the attitude psychological possessed by each individual trader or by any other active subject present on the market with respect to fundamental factors. Naturally an expanding economy favors the performance of stock prices, on the other hand a downward economy leads to an increase in the level of bond prices, while an inflationary phase favors some commodities, such as gold and all values related to it. These three markets, in an attempt to anticipate three different situations, move in opposite directions at the same time, showing all the instability of the financial world.

In reality, therefore, a stable economy can rarely be observed, ie an economy floating around an imaginary median line, known as an equilibrium line. Coinciding with the equilibrium line, economic growth would be null, that is neither in expansion nor in recession. But precisely because of the large number of forces that act on it and influence its movement and evolution, the economy can never be identified at the theoretical equilibrium line. Depending on the stage of maturation of the financial market, some elements show an upward trend, supported by a strong intensity, while other elements could show a downward trend, to then exchange roles in other market phases. Traders themselves would never want the financial market to stretch for long periods on the equilibrium line, as during these phases it is much more difficult to make profits. Every investor, in addition to following a specific trend, tries to identify what may be a maximum point or a minimum point of the price level, because it is precisely by anticipating a possible reversal of the trend that the best profits can be obtained. At the same time, as the trend moves away from its equilibrium line, it becomes more and more unstable and, beyond a certain level, the probabilities that it can reverse the evolution of its evolution from one moment to another increase more and more.

If the distance that separates the trend from its equilibrium line is wide, the force imparted to its course once the trend is reversed is considered almost proportional to the one that has led it upwards and therefore it is likely to reach a point of minimum equidistant from the equilibrium line as the maximum point just touched. Generally, however, the expanding phases have a longer duration than the recession periods. Bulls and bears, considered the active subjects par excellence, attempt to exploit the various upward and downward periods of the various markets, such as the stock market, the gold market and the bond market, focusing their strategies also on the duration of each phase. However, each of these markets shows a correlation with the theoretical economic cycle, with expansionary and recessive phases that are different from each other, also due to the behavior implemented by bulls and bears, who buy and sell their positions trying to exploit the different evolutions of the price trends.

Once a minimum point has been reached within the bond market, the economy enters a recession, and investors realize that the trend may soon turn around and, for this reason, open up positions. , giving way to the recovery. This recovery has the consequence of increasing the inflation rate and therefore the gold market in turn reverses the trend, going from a downward phase to an upward one. The achievement of a minimum point in the bond market, therefore, involves a phase during which all markets are upward. This scenario, however, has a very short duration: in fact, the upside phase also concerns interest rates, which are inversely proportional to the bonds. This means that an ascending phase of the economy involves reaching a maximum point in the bond market, with the consequent reversal of the trend. All other markets, on the other hand, continue in their ascending phase, as the asset has excess capital and labor. Investors, however, will soon realize that the economy is running out of intensity and profits will tend to shrink for them: it no longer makes sense for them to leave their positions open in the market and, closing them, will resume the downward trend of the trend until the stock market reaches a new low point.

1.5 – The various theories of Technical Analysis

Today's Technical Analysis is the result of a series of theories and techniques developed over the years, which have been slowly optimized and adapted to evolving markets, in order to obtain ever better results, able to reduce the level of risk and increase that of performance.

Ralph Nelson Elliot, during the early years of the 20th century, gave birth to a theory founded on the concept that market oscillations are not the result of chance. According to Elliot, in fact, the market tends to follow behaviors, or real laws, based on Fibonacci's golden idea. Elliot's hypothesis was truly innovative, as it meant that it was possible to make predictions about future market trends. Price fluctuations, ie upward and downward developments, follow the "wave" sequence in a constant and almost monotonous manner. In his theory, Elliot also created a standard structure of market trends, composed of five waves, which follow the direction of the primary trend, and three other waves, of smaller size and duration, which follow an opposite direction from the first and which have the function of correcting the price level.

Over the years other theorists, including Miner, Prechter and Frost have imposed some rules, concerning the strength, duration and direction of the trend, to try to refine the entire theory of Elliot. In reality this theory, in order to have a good chance of success, must be accompanied and supported by further indicators and oscillators, capable of picking up signals from the market and providing the investor with a more solid basis for market analysis.

In addition to the Elliot theory, the Technical Analysis is also based on the 24 rules of Gann's theory. William D. Gann was one of the most well-known traders in the entire history of the financial market, as by implementing his trading technique he managed to succeed in the darkest economic moment, ie during the Great Depression, implementing his own capital of about 50 million dollars.

Gann has based his trading activity on precise rules, twenty-four, which guarantee a wide probability of success. With his technique Gann, starting in 1933, opened 479 operations, winning 422, increasing the allocated capital by more than 4000%. The incredible numbers obtained by Gann have led millions of traders over the years to study its bases and to adopt the rules established in his theory. Today many Trading Systems, or automated trading systems, can be used by setting all the twenty-four rules of Gann's theory, so that the system can open and close positions with a greater probability of success.

William Gann has included his rules in the book "45 Years in Wall Street", published in 1949. In addition to the rules, this text also contains many other tips that Gann has decided to spread to all traders. He also elaborated one of the most formidable tools of the stock market, known as Gann's range, which allows to analyze in detail the trend of the financial instruments.

Even today, despite the profound transformation that has involved both the financial markets and the instruments traded in it, also due to the increasingly accentuated globalization that has influenced the entire economic world and which has allowed traders to appear en masse on the markets of scholarship, the twenty-four rules of Gann's theory are still valid.

Investors who decide to adopt this trading method are guaranteed to have a solid base on which to base their Technical Analysis strategy, which in turn must be coordinated on the basis of the previously established objectives.

Gann based his theory on the in-depth study of historical series, but also on the analysis of the cyclical nature of the events that can directly or indirectly influence the financial market. In order to fully understand it, however, it is necessary to read carefully the entire statement proposed by Gann and it would not be enough to quickly observe the rules and then dive into trading and hope to get profits quickly.

Naturally, however, the theory that has been most successful within the trading world is the one conceived by Dow, which is considered the real principle on which Technical Analysis has based its roots.

Chapter 2 - Dow's Theory

The most important and ancient theory of Technical Analysis is Dow's Theory, which all traders should know. The origins of this theory date back to 1882, when Charles Dow founded, together with Edward Jones, a company called Dow Jones & Co., introducing in 1884 a fundamental stock market index still today for the analysis of the American financial market, the well-known Dow Jones Industrial. Dow was also the founder of one of the largest financial newspapers in the world, the Wall Street Journal, in which he published a series of articles to explain the trend of financial markets through the use of charts, expressing his vision of the stock market. He was the first to focus his attention on the behavior of the investor to make future forecasts on possible market cycles.

However, his theories were never collected until several years after his death: in 1932, in fact, a book was published called Dow Theory, which turned out to be a real economic theory, which created the conditions for the development of Technical analysis of financial markets.

The Dow Theory is based on the analysis of the world economy and the market, in order to accurately assess the direction that the stock or trend will take. Thanks to this theory, indices have been created to estimate the economic conditions of companies in the industrial and railway sectors, specifically the Dow Jones Industrial and the Dow Jones Index Rail Index, currently called the Transportation Index, but almost all of the concepts expressed from this theory they are also applicable to the other indices. The Theory of Dow continues to be still the basis of the Technical Analysis, after more than 100 years from its conception.

2.1 – The six fundamental points of Dow's Theory

Dow's Theory is based on six basic principles, identifiable in the assumption that the stock price index reflects the emotions and decisions taken by all the players on the stock market, through a process that discounts all that could affect some way on the supply and demand on the stock exchange. So the six principles can be listed as follows: prices discount everything, the market consists of three trends, the primary trend is divided into three phases, market indices must confirm each other, the volume must confirm the trend, the trend is in place until a definitive inversion signal is displayed.

2.1.1 – Prices discount everything

The first point in Dow's Theory states that prices discount everything that can affect demand and supply in the stock market. Therefore the prerequisite is to assimilate in the prices all those elements that cannot be foreseen in advance. In fact, it is enough a new news or a voice to destabilize the market, which must however be able to adapt and incorporate every event, adapting the price.

Therefore it is possible to affirm that the market assimilates everything that concerns it at the very moment in which the information becomes known, therefore traders will not have to read up on the events that could affect it. With each external change the stock market regulates itself, through a new assessment.

This principle is at the basis of Technical Analysis, but it does not mean that traders should not in any case have the fundamental competences relative to the market and when it is appropriate or not to open a position, as otherwise they could incur substantial losses of capital.

2.1.2 – The market has three trends

The second principle of Dow's Theory assumes that the stock market has three tendencies, the primary movement, the secondary reactions and the minor movements, which differ above all for duration.

The primary movement or trend is the most important and its tendency can last from one year up to several years. Its trend can be upward, so-called bullish, or downward, so-called bearish. In the first case, the market players are the bulls, which move when prices reach decreasing minimums and maximums, in the down-trend phase of the market. In the second case, the market players are bears, which act when prices reach increasing minimums and maximums, and the market is therefore in an up-trend phase.

Secondary or intermediate reactions or trends move contrary to the primary trend and represent corrective phases. So if the main trend is upward, secondary trends will be down or they will constitute correction or consolidation phases, vice versa if the primary trend is downward, secondary tendencies will be upward or may constitute lateral settlement phases. This type of trend usually has an average duration ranging from three weeks to three months. Secondary retracements are usually between 1/3 and 2/3 of the main trend, and are characterized by a higher degree of volatility.

The third movement of the market is represented by the minor trend, which has a duration of less than three weeks. This tendency normally includes the corrective movements of the secondary trend or the movements opposite to it. Given the short duration, this movement is not recognized as fundamental by the supporters of Dow Theory, who actually use it to get an overview of the market along with the other two trends. Analyzing the minor trends is in fact very risky, as you could have a non-rational view of the market that would affect the way you trade.

2.1.3 – The primary trend has three phases

The third point of Dow's Theory is based on the assumption that the primary trend has three phases, namely the accumulation phase, the participation phase and the distribution phase.

The accumulation phase arises following purchases by more informed and more astute investors, when they believe that the market has already assimilated all the negative news. In a market with an upward trend, this phase coincides with the point at which the beginning of the upward trend occurred, ie with the minimum of a downward trend in most cases. In the case of a bull market, the accumulation phase is complex to identify, as it can be exchanged with simple oscillations within a given range, but Technical Analysis can facilitate this identification, thanks to the fact that this phase can be preceded by a phase in which there is the consolidation of a previous downward trend. The market is therefore in a lateral phase and those who do not have sufficient information prefer to be cautious and not invest, thus generating unimportant price differences, as few are those who invest, the so-called big players.

In the second phase, that of participation, trend followers expose themselves by taking a position, so prices rise, generating a certain euphoria among investors, even among the most skeptical. Thus public participation in the market has increased, thanks to the positive news. However, when the maximum peak is reached, the third phase will be passed, as there will be no more investors willing to buy.

The third phase, namely that of distribution, also known as the excess phase, begins precisely when the most cunning and experienced investors begin to limit their investments to avoid losing the profit obtained. Thus, there is a reversal of the trend, with the consequent fall in prices and a considerable decline in confidence in the market, which turns into real "panic" among savers. Unlike the big players, in this phase the smaller retail traders will enter the market, in a cycle of purchases and sales in the hope of making a profit, until the price collapses to its minimum. Once the minimum is reached, the market re-establishes itself and returns to the first phase of the trend.

2.1.4 – Market indices must confirm each other

According to Dow's theory the indexes present on the market, similar to each other, must be correlated to each other to be subject to the same economic conditions, thus confirming each other. According to this theory, no upward or downward signal can in fact occur if there is no correlation between the Dow Jones Industrial index and the Dow Jones Transportation index: only if both indices exceed a certain maximum will one find oneself of facing a real bullish trend, or vice versa in the case of a downward trend.

If there is a difference between the two indices, then there will be a change in the tendency of one of the two, while if there is correlation the two indices do nothing but confirm each other.

2.1.5 – The volume must confirm the trend

When downward or upward trends are accompanied by significant volumes, the strength of the trends is confirmed according to Dow Theory. If, on the other hand, the volumes are relatively low, the trend continues to be valid, but is unable to show the complete picture of the market. In fact, according to Dow, volumes accompany price movements, acting as indicators. The volume is a secondary indicator which, confirming the change in price, confirms the trend. So if prices fall or rise, the volume must grow, indicating the increase in the number of subjects taking a position in the market.

2.1.6 – The trend is in progress until a definitive inversion signal appears

Until a definitive reversal signal appears, the trend remains in place. Therefore, investors follow the primary trend taking place in the financial market, carefully analyzing price fluctuations, with the aim of making the most of the movements that go in the same direction as the main trend followed. In fact these oscillations are more extensive than the consolidation and correction pauses that may occur. These phases of fluctuation represent the best time for investments, as the risk / return ratio is very favorable, especially in cases where we operate through trend following. If the main trend is downwards, traders evaluate the opportunities to exit the market or sell short in the short term, but if the main trend is upward, traders consider buying opportunities with a low level of risk in the long run.

2.2 – Bulls and bears in the financial market

In the stock market language the names of two animals are used to identify two distinct categories of investors, namely bulls and bears.

The term bull indicates a rising market, in which investors are called bullish, and denotes the positive trend of the market. The term bear instead identifies a market characterized by pessimism that leads to phases of decline, in which investors are called bearish. The origin of the two terms is to be found in the ways in which these two animals attack their prey, with the horns upwards the bull and with the claws downwards the bear.

2.2.1 – *The bulls*

The bull market is also called bullish, and defines a market with upward trends, which encourages traders to invest, with determination and optimism. So when the market is in this phase it is characterized by a strong positivity. The bull market phase can last for long periods of time, registering positive results and profits. Investing your capital at this stage can be very profitable, but in the long run it can lead the market to form so-called speculative bubbles, characterized by a noticeable price increase without real reasons, due to the increase in demand over a period of time limited. If the value of the securities collapses rapidly, the speculative bubble bursts and investors will lose all the money invested. According to Dow's theory, after the bubble burst phase the cycle will restart from the first accumulation phase, in which the market will return to moderately growth. So bullish markets are characterized by very strong demand and a weak supply, so there are many who would like to buy but not as many those who are willing to sell, with the consequent increase in prices.

2.2.2 – Bears

Unlike the bull market, the bear market is at a time of pessimism and negative results, with a downward trend in assets. This type of market is also called bearish and those who invest in this phase obtain profits from the open downward transactions. The bearish markets are characterized by the presence of continuous price retracements, which fall below the real value of the securities, due to the confusion and fear that is spreading among the less experienced small investors who try to close the open positions even at cost to suffer heavy losses. The bear market phase is in most cases the starting point for the bull phase, as after reaching the minimum levels the market will rise again, according to the principles of Dow's Theory, thanks to the intervention of more investors experts and daring that will ensure that "the bear goes into hibernation" to make room for a new bullish phase.

Chapter 3 - Graphs, oscillators and indicators of Technical Analysis

In order to use the principles of Technical Analysis fruitfully, each trader must rely on some tools that will make trading easier and less random.

First of all, investors will have to use some charts able to faithfully report in real time what is happening in the financial market and the fluctuations in the prices of financial instruments traded by the various parties.

In addition to the charts there are also oscillators and indicators. In reality these instruments can be considered both indicators, but there is a characteristic that distinguishes the oscillators. In fact the latter move in a certain range, oscillating around a line, and are very useful during the lateral phases of the market. Conversely, indicators tend to follow the trend directly, constantly focusing and following the price. Precisely for this reason the indicators are recommended during the tendential phases, especially those in which the push that moves the trend is strong and intense.

Each tool will allow the technical analyst to deepen the studies on the market, but also to pick up the signals coming from it, so as to have greater chances of success. It should not be forgotten, however, that Technical Analysis turns its attention especially to individual prices and their evolutions, therefore these instruments must be used only as an aid to the study carried out and not as the only elements to be used.

In general, the purpose of graphs, oscillators and indicators is to identify a trend, to understand its entity and, consequently, to guess what its actual duration may be before it reaches a maximum point and reverses its orientation.

3.1 – The most important graphs

The technical analyst uses the charts to get an immediate view of the market trend. An experienced trader is able to immediately detect the presence of any critical points, which involve market hesitations, and the entry or exit of the trend from areas considered particularly advantageous for trading purposes. The graph also shows which of the two active market players, buyers or sellers, has more strength in a given moment and how the demand curve and the supply curve move. If the demand appears much stronger than the offer, the trader can identify the support points. The prices, at this level, are excessively low and therefore it is possible to assume a probable rise in the trend. For this reason the supports often coincide with the lows, in particular with the historical lows, which represent the lowest value recorded by the price of a particular financial instrument in a time interval that can be more or less wide.

On the other hand, resistance represents the level at which the offer prevails over demand. The trend turns towards areas where prices are excessively high and therefore will certainly be corrected to the downside. The most important point of resistance coincides with the historical maximum, a level beyond which the trend will hardly be able to go again.

It is possible to distinguish, according to their function, two different types of graphs: those of inversion and those of continuation.

3.1.1 – The inversion figures

Following a particularly long-lasting trend, it is possible to observe the formation of an inversion figure within a graph. The inversion assumes that the observed trend has lost the strength and intensity necessary to be able to continue its directional trend, and therefore will soon reverse its trend. The inversion generally takes place in particular modes, which bring the price line to form well-defined figures that are easily identifiable by traders.

The most well-known inversion figure is certainly the so-called Head and shoulders. This is created by three distinct phases. The first is generally composed of an upward trend, with very strong volumes, which is immediately corrected by a bearish trend, with decidedly lower volumes. An inverted V will then appear on the graph which will constitute the left shoulder of the figure. The second phase begins again with a bullish trend and with the exceeding of the previous highs, but the volumes do not increase and soon the trend will slide downwards, taking on a downward trend again. The minimum point of this new upside-down V, wider than the first, will be positioned near the minimum of the left shoulder. The third phase is represented by a further V similar to the first, but which presents lower volumes and prices. This figure will form the right shoulder, following a hypothetical neck line. This line shows what the orientation of the trend is and to identify it, it will be enough to join the points of connection between the neck and the left shoulder and between the neck and the right shoulder by means of a segment.

The real reversal will take place following another small bullish phase, leaving time for the traders to observe the correct completion of the figure and to carry out their investment, before the price value falls dramatically. At this point the neck line will become a resistance that the trader must necessarily take into account. Of course if the trend is down the whole figure will appear upside down, while the three Vs, which form the head and the two shoulders, will be the right way this time.

A second inversion figure is represented by the so-called double minimum or double maximum. This figure represents the situation in which a trend, be it bullish or bearish, will reach the same price level twice, but without ever managing to go further: these levels represent the maximum points, if the trend is upward, or minimum points, if the trend is downward.

Once the figure is finished, the trend will reverse its trend. The second maximum or minimum point may have values slightly lower or slightly higher than the first point, respectively, but this does not mean that you are not in the presence of an inversion figure. If for the figure Head and shoulders the analyst had to trace the triple V, with the central one larger than the lateral ones, in this case it is necessary to identify an M, which will be straight in case of double maximum and reversed in the case of double minimum . Sometimes, however, the maximums and minimums could even be three, and therefore we will talk about triple maximum and minimum triple. The technical analyst must in any case take into consideration the value of the volumes referred to the observed financial instrument.

The Top Reversal or Spike represents the third figure of inversion in order of importance. This is formed following a sudden upward trend followed by a downward trend of the same entity that brings the figure back to the initial price level. Subsequently, the trend will definitively reverse its trend. The main feature is that the completion of the figure occurs in a rather short period of time:

generally it concerns secondary trends, while only rarely is identified on primary trends. Furthermore, the Top Reversals are anticipated by an unjustified increase in market volumes, a sign that the trader must be able to correctly understand to be able to make profits.

3.1.2 – The continuation figures

The continuation figures identify in a graph the moments of pause of the trend following which, the trend will probably resume its trend. These figures are therefore indispensable as they allow the technical analyst to identify the probable evolution of the observed trend. It is therefore essential to understand how long the slowdown in the trend can last before resuming the trend, and to do so the analyst is confronted with various figures.

The simplest continuation figure to recognize is certainly the triangle. There are three different triangle models, namely the ascending one, the descending one and the symmetrical one. Everyone generally precedes a sudden change in the price level, be it upward or downward, which can be caused by a change in volatility in a very short period of time. The triangle, however, is an ambiguous figure because, although it is generally succeeded by a continuation of the trend, it can sometimes even anticipate a reversal of the trend. The ascending triangles allow to identify a series of increasing maximums and minimums, while the descending ones identify points of maximums and minimums that follow a hypothetical decreasing line. In both cases the next trend will follow the trend undertaken by price levels. As for asymmetric triangles, which identify a trend composed of minimums and maximums of ever lower value, thus forming a sort of cone shape, the identification of the future trend may appear more complicated. To anticipate the trend it is therefore necessary to analyze both the trend preceding the formation of the figure and the values of the volumes present on the market.

Another rectangle widely used by traders and technical analysts is the rectangle. This outlines the entire congestion area that entails the trend slowdown before the trend resumes. The price trend reaches a series of maximums and minimums enclosed in a horizontal range. Traders can make profits either by investing in the recovery of the trend undertaken by the price level before entering the congested area, or by buying positions in the minimum points to resell them in the maximum points.

The wedges or wedges are figures of continuation similar to the triangles, but which assume an exit from the figure with opposite tendential orientation with respect to that of entry. Compared to triangles, however, the wedge takes a longer time to complete and therefore requires a more in-depth study by analysts.

Other continuation figures are the flags and pennants, respectively flags and pennants. These figures identify a very short series of maxima and minima, with narrow and rapid oscillations, which follow an inverse trend with respect to the initial trend and which continue on the same trend as the latter. Being very fast, the flags and pennants require a constant presence of the analyst on the market, so as to make rapid investments once the figure is completed.

3.2 – The main technical oscillators

Oscillators can be considered a sub-category of indicators, but they still represent a very important tool for technical analysts and for traders especially if used during the so-called lateral phases of the market, ie during those phases in which it is not possible to identify a real trend and therefore it is much more difficult to obtain profits. Compared to the indicators, these instruments do not directly follow the trend, but rather oscillate within a range, sending signals to the trader when the probability that the trend reverses its trend increases. There are a number of oscillators that the trader can use, depending on his attitude within the market, but also according to the objectives he intends to achieve. The main and most used oscillators are the moving averages, the Momentum, the stochastic oscillator, the Bollinger bands, the RSI and the MACD.

3.2.1 – The moving averages

Moving averages are probably the type of oscillator most used by traders worldwide. In addition to its ease of use and extreme flexibility, the moving average makes it possible to derive from the oscillations a much smoother line than the price level that helps to identify the true trend to follow. There are three different models of moving averages, namely the simple one, which guarantees objectivity in the consideration of the individual prices analyzed, the exponential one, which instead focuses attention on the most recent prices, and the weighted one, which gives greater importance to the more recent values price, but does so while also taking into account the older values.

3.2.2 – The Momentum

A second oscillator widely used by traders and fundamental for Technical Analysis is the Momentum. This has the task of analyzing the intensity or the speed of the trend, taking into consideration the price value at a given moment and comparing it with its past value. One of the main features of the Momentum is that this instrument does not act, like almost every other oscillator, within a positive range, but also operates on the negative elements caused by the presence of bearish trends. The Momentum launches signals when the oscillation reaches the zero line: these signals are bullish if the oscillator passes from negative values to positive values, while they are bearish in the opposite case.

3.2.3 – The stochastic oscillator

The stochastic oscillator, conceived by George Lane in the second half of the 20th century, is an oscillator that acts on the basis of two curves, defined as% K and% D. The first of these two curves is obtained on the graph considering the percentage given by the ratio between a given closing price of the observed trend and the values recorded by the same price in a previous time interval. The second curve is nothing more than the moving average of the% K curve. Analyzing these two curves on the market, the oscillator is able to understand when the trend is about to reach a maximum point or a minimum point, thus sending signals to the trader.

3.2.4 – The Bollinger bands

The Bollinger bands are represented graphically by three lines, the first oscillating above the trend, the second below it, while the third, central, represents an average of the price values.

If the trend should touch or exceed the upper band, the market is considered in an overbought area, and most likely the price will tend to go down shortly; vice versa, if the trend will breach the lower band, then an oversold situation is created, so the price will soon rise.

The upper line is therefore considered a resistance, while the lower one is a support.

3.2.5 – Relative Strength Index (RSI)

The Relative Strength Index oscillator, better known as RSI, provides signals similar to those launched by Bollinger bands, but bases its action on two lines, in a range between 20 and 80. If the moving average should overrun the upper value of the range, then we are in the presence of an overbought situation, vice versa if the lower limit is raised it means that the trend has entered an oversold zone.

However, it is essential that the RSI oscillator is not used individually. This in fact must necessarily follow a moving average in order to be able to launch signals. Furthermore, the RSI can provide excellent results when combined with the Bollinger bands, a combination used by most traders.

3.2.6 – Moving Average Convergence-Divergence (MACD)

The MACD oscillator, or Moving Average Convergence-Divergence, allows you to combine several basic principles of Technical Analysis. The MACD bases its approach on the calculation and representation of two moving averages, calculated taking into consideration different time intervals, and on their difference. One of the two moving averages will be faster than the other, and the signal of a trend change will be launched as soon as the two lines cross. If the slower line were to follow the new trend drawn by the faster line, then the reliability of the signal can be considered almost certain.

It is a widespread and widely used oscillator, both for its excellent results and for its simplicity.

3.3 – Market indicators

Indicators are the tools that guarantee the best results when used in the presence of a trend.

In fact, they tend to pursue, almost obstinately, the trend undertaken by the market, without trying to anticipate a possible trend reversal.

3.3.1 – Advance-Decline Line (AD Line)

The Advance-Decline Line indicators, also known more simply as the AD Line, allow you to analyze the data of individual financial products, subdividing the upward and downward securities, and discarding the unchanged ones from the previous days. In this way the trader can have a clear view of the trends on the market and their intensity, so as to be able to apply their strategy correctly.

This indicator can be used on any type of market, even on that of commodities.

3.3.2 – Advance-Decline Volume Line

The Advance-Decline Volume Line is an indicator that analyzes the various volumes of the individual assets, in order to provide important indications in relation to the intensity of the trends.

It is used in combination with the AD Line: the AD Volume Line, in fact, calculates the net progress volume and adds it to the results provided by the AD Line, in order to identify the tendential strength.

3.3.3 – McClellan's indicator

The McClellan indicator is used to understand which direction the trend is taking. This launches the signals, when the line of the indicator intersects with the line of moving averages, or when the market finds itself in areas of overbought and oversold.

It is often combined with the MACD oscillator, in order to obtain more precise indications.

3.3.4 – The Arms indicator (Trin)

The Arms indicator, also known as Trin, is a very important tool, as it is used by technical analysts to understand if the volume of the market is the result of an exchange that mainly concerns securities with a bearish trend, or securities with a bullish trend .

If the value of the indicator is above 1.0, then the instrument will launch bearish signals, while if the value is less than 1.0, it will launch bullish signals.

3.3.5 – Volatility Index (VIX)

Using the VIX indicator, or Volatility Index, it is possible to calculate the expected volatility on the market, with a forecast that can reach a maximum interval of thirty days. To obtain an estimate of this kind, the Volatility Index makes a weighted average of the volatility related to the prices of each individual financial market option. Understanding what the future volatility of an asset may be is fundamental, as it allows you to optimize the relationship between return and risk of your capital management strategy.

3.3.6 – Put/Call Ratio

The Put / Call Ratio is an indicator that seeks market sentiment, separating the buyers from the sellers in the analysis carried out within the same. In this way the trader can understand what the volume of open trades is, that is put operations, and the volume of open transactions to the upside, or call transactions.

Conclusions

The keys to the success of the Technical Analysis therefore lie in two concepts: knowledge and action. The study of the market must be accompanied by a timely investment, with a just allocation of capital, which must neither be excessively high nor excessively low.

The correct application of the assumptions, however, is sometimes not sufficient to guarantee success within the financial market. Traders generally commit errors that can diminish the effectiveness of the

Technical Analysis, generating unexpected losses.

The most common mistake made by the trader lies in the desire to obtain profits in the very short term. The interpreted indicators look to the long term, as the analyzed trends can last even several years. If the results provided by these tools are applied to very short-term trends, then the outcome will certainly be negative.

Another mistake is to focus one's attention only on one or two indicators. In fact, each indicator shows its strengths if applied during a particular market phase and above all if combined with the action of other instruments.

The emotion is another element that must be estranged during the course of the trading activity. The technical analyst must be able to remain humble during the positive phases and not give up during the negative ones. He must never be carried away by the desire to immediately recover a loss, but he must always try to remain rational and objective. To do so it can also rely on automated trading systems, known as Trading Systems.

Of course to succeed in the world of trading it is not enough to follow the majority. If a signal indicates an event contrary to that expected by most market participants, the technical analyst is required to follow it, without considering what the other investors are doing.

Implementing a complex and convoluted strategy can be counterproductive. The assumptions of the Technical Analysis are simple in themselves, and the same simplicity must be reported within one's trading strategy. Complexity is in fact a source of errors, sometimes even trivial, that can send the whole analysis to the air.

Finally, the last common error concerns the intention to analyze and anticipate every single oscillation of the market. Being able to achieve success by acting in this way is almost impossible. It is in fact necessary to identify only the main points that may concern a turning point, a pause or a continuation of the trend.

Only once all these concepts have been assimilated will the technical analyst be able to act objectively on the market and generate ever greater profits, thus achieving success in the financial market.

www.ingramcontent.com/pod-product-compliance
Lightning Source LLC
Chambersburg PA
CBHW072030230526
45466CB00020B/1334